up Against the Wall

Jawanza Kunjufu
Lady June Hubbard

Original Screenplay

Emma Young

Songodina Ifatunji

Chuck Colbert

Zuindi Colbert

IMAGES
African American Images
Chicago, Illinois

First Edition
Third Printing 1991

Copyright © 1991 by Jawanza Kunjufu

Photo Credits: Bill Taylor

There was an air of excitement on the Hamilton High School track. Today was tryout day for the team. The group for the cross-country event had warmed up and gathered near the starting point. Sean had waited all year for this day. He was new to the school this year, and he knew track was the one thing that would make him feel right at home. The coach and his assistant, Mr. Wilkes, knew of Sean's reputation for being the top runner in the city, when he was in junior high. They both had made it clear that he would have to prove himself in the tryouts today to make the team. He was a little nervous. He knew he was up against some tough competition, and he wasn't sure just how well he'd be accepted by the team, if he made it. He'd never been in a predominately white environment before, and had been trying to adjust. He was never quite relaxed because he wasn't legitimately attending the school. His older brother Jesse lived in the neighborhood, so Sean used his address to attend the school, but actually commuted daily from the projects across town.

Jason Roberts, known as J.R., was standing with his buddy, Steve. He was known for his remarkable performance in track, but he also was known for making derogatory remarks about people of color. J.R. shook his long, blonde hair and pulled it back into a rubber band. Steve laughed.

"You know, Coach is going to make you get a haircut J.R."

"Yeah I know. But I've got time." J.R. pointed towards Sean who was talking to Mr. Wilkes' son, Kevin. Kevin was built like his father, but on a smaller scale. They were both muscular and compact, and had bronze-colored skin.

"Looks like Kevin is trying to make the team a little darker. He's brought one of his jungle companions to tryout."

Steve looked. "Yeah, but he looks kind of small. What do you think, J.R.?"

"Hey, there's no telling with those Nee-groes. They spend their whole childhood running from the police! Size doesn't mean a thing. Let's hope a siren doesn't go off while we're running, or they're likely to break a school record!" They both laughed and moved toward the group.

The coach blew his whistle and began calling names through the bullhorn. Everyone moved toward the starting line as their names were called. After the twenty-five youths were assembled, the gun was fired and the race began. The group took off and quickly began to break into small groups. They all knew they had to save their speed for the final portion of the run.

J.R. and Steve moved to the front of the pack at a steady pace, followed by Kevin and then Sean. The path was headed for a wooded area. As J.R. passed Kevin and Sean, he muttered a comment.

"We've got to go through the woods up here, don't you boys get to thinking that you're back in the jungle now."

"We won't." Kevin replied as he took the lead. "As long as you and your pet chimpanzee, don't start your swinging through the trees on a vine routine."

Sean smiled but concentrated on his pace. He didn't want to burn out too soon. Sean had been running most of his life. As he ran, he began to remember running in the projects. Usually, it was just a case of being in the wrong place at the wrong time. He remembered being chased by some older boys from a playground, because someone else had knocked one of their bicycles over. One of them had picked up a thick piece of wood, and another had something shiny in his hand that looked like a knife. Sean had run as fast and as hard as he could. He was able to outrun them and made it home safely.

On another occasion, he stopped by a friend's place after school. It was an old, dark tenement building. He knew it was always better to walk through the building in pairs, but Sean walked himself that day. As he reached the third floor, someone called for him to help them. He hesitated and then went to see what the woman wanted. When he reached her, two more hookers stepped out of the shadows. Their eyes were glazed and he could smell alcohol on their breath. They had mumbled something about "fresh, tender meat" and started pulling at his shirt and belt buckle. Sean was frightened. He swung his arms and tried to kick at them, but they dodged his efforts and said they "might have to tie this one down." When he felt his belt buckle give away, he took a deep breath and jerked and kicked with all his might. He fell away from two of them but someone still was holding on to his sleeve. He grabbed her wrist and bit it as hard as he could. The woman yelled, and Sean broke loose. He jumped down the rest of the steps with two of the hookers stumbling down behind him. They were cursing and threatening to kill his little black....

Sean felt his muscles tensing. Realizing where he was now, he had to adjust his pace again. He had been so engrossed in his memories, he had actually increased his pace. He could see J.R. and Kevin ahead of him, turning the bend back toward the school. He still had a bit of a way to go, and he knew he had to relax and keep his arms low like Coach had emphasized. He would slowly increase his speed after a few more strides and then really turn it on.

Sean soon found his mind wandering again. This time, he remembered picking up some shoes in a brown paper bag from his mother's friend. As he left her apartment, he decided to take a shortcut through an alley. Just as he reached the end, he ran into a policeman's billy club. The officers had been called to a robbery in the building next to the alley. So, when Sean came running down the alley with a paper bag in hand, he was met with a club to his stomach. He dropped the bag and crumpled to the ground. The blow had knocked the air out of him. He felt his legs quivering beneath him.

Sean inhaled deeply. He was back on the track at school. He could hear people yelling and cheering, but he couldn't go on. He didn't have the strength. He felt himself bending over and gasping for air.

"Come on Sean, you can do it!" The coach was standing with Mr. Wilkes at the finish line. "Don't give up Sean! Keep running!" Somehow Sean managed to cross the line.

"You made it Sean. You did it!" Mr. Wilkes was holding a stopwatch and a towel.

"You mean I won?" Sean gasped.

"I mean you won a place on the team. You just made the team."

"But what happened, Coach? I thought I was going to pass out. I almost collapsed."

"You hit the wall, Sean."

"Hit the wall. Hit what wall?"

"That's what happens when you get to the point where you feel like you just can't go any further. In track, it's like your lungs and your legs have turned to lead, and you feel like you can't take another step or breath. It happens all the time in life. Things happen, and it can get to the point where you feel like you're at rock bottom with nowhere to go. Then things work out, you move forward and you look back on it as a lesson. In track, you're going to learn about your wall and how to get past it. We'll talk more about it later. Go on to the locker room. "

Kevin had finished right behind Sean. Sean walked over to him and slapped him on the back. "Alright man, we did it!"

"Yeah man, looks like it's you and me."

Just then, two girls came running up to the boys. Lisa Roberts was J.R.'s younger sister and had a crush on Kevin. She was petite, with thick brown hair. Her features were dark in contrast to her brother's. She handed Kevin a towel and flashed her straight white teeth. Her best friend was Denise Taylor, one of the most popular girls in the school. Denise was bright, beautiful, and very anxious to meet Sean. Her copper brown complexion was flawless, and the mane of curls framed her face perfectly.

"Hey, you guys were great, Kevin! You came in right behind my brother."

Denise was eyeing Sean.

"Who's your friend Kev? Why don't you introduce us? I heard Coach call him Sean at the finish line."

"Not now, ladies. We've got to catch our breath." Kevin put an arm around Sean and they headed into the locker room.

"Well, I'm Denise. Congratulations, Sean."

"I'm Lisa. You were great, Sean!"

Sean glanced over his shoulder just before the door closed. Denise winked and waved. Sean smiled.

At their lockers Sean and Kevin could hear someone congratulating J.R., and telling him that his best friend Steve didn't make the team. J.R. slammed his locker.

"Steve would be on the team if that new tar baby had stayed in the projects in the welfare line."

"You know," Kevin raised his voice to make sure J.R. heard him. "There are 35 million people on welfare and, out of that, 23 million are white. Check it out the next time your uncles and cousins go to pick up their welfare checks."

"Don't push me Kevin."

Kevin and Sean laughed and headed for the showers. When they were dressed and back outside, Mr. Wilkes patted both boys on the back.

"I'm really proud of you two."

"Thanks, Mr. Wilkes." Sean was beaming.

"You know Sean, my dad made it to the Olympic Trials in track."

"Hey, cool, Mr. Wilkes." Mr. Wilkes smiled and puffed out his chest.

"Yes, and I see some real championship potential in you too Sean."

Mr. Wilkes turned around and called his other son, Darryl, over. Darryl recognized Sean right away.

"Yo, bro, you did a real number on them today. I remember seeing your picture in the paper a while back. Where did you train?"

"Train?" Sean had to think for a minute. "I guess the streets trained me. I was always told not to fight, so in order to survive, I ran."

The Wilkes men looked at each other and started laughing. Kevin spoke first.

"Wait a minute, man. Are you telling me you don't throw down? A brother from the 'hood and you don't thump?"

Sean shrugged, "That's right. But from some of the vibes I'm getting around here, I may have walked from the frying pan and into the fire."

Darryl and Mr. Wilkes looked confused. Kevin clarified it for them.

"Sean had his first encounter with J.R. and Steve today."

"Hey I'm not used to the environment yet, not to mention having some white boys crackin' on me!"

Darryl put his hands on his hips and nodded.

"Destiny. War in the heavens. Opposition in your astral chart. Your ancestors have guided you here to fulfill your rites of passage, Sean. It's your destiny."

"Rites of passage?"

"Your journey into manhood brother. This is a different kind of front, with all kinds of obstacles to face. It doesn't matter if you go over or around, just as long as you get to the other side."

Kevin shook his head, "Yeah O.K. Darryl, give us a break. He does that to everyone I introduce to him, Sean."

"It's cool with me, Kev. It sounds kind of interesting actually."

Mr. Wilkes took out his car keys.

"Anybody feel like grabbing some pizza?"

"Sure." Kevin responded.

Darryl nodded,"I'm right behind you. Just ask them to make one half of it meatless. What do you say, Sean?"

"Sounds good, Mr. Wilkes. But I'd better be going. I'm sure my mother is waiting to hear what happened."

"O.K., Sean, Darryl, why don't you give him a ride home?"

"No, that's alright." Sean protested. "I can make it."

"No problem kid. I'll take you home. That's me over there." Darryl pointed. "The little blue car with the rust spots."

Sean had to think fast. He didn't want the Wilkes to know he didn't live in the neighborhood. He decided to let Darryl take him to his brother's house.

"O.K., let's go. Thanks anyway, Mr. Wilkes. Kevin, I'll catch up with you tomorrow." Sean followed Darryl to his car and waved to Mr. Wilkes and Kevin. He directed Darryl to his brother's house. As they pulled up to the house, Darryl looked surprised.

"Wait a minute, man. Are you telling me you and your mother live here? Since when?"

"Well," Sean started.

"Naw, man. Nobody's home here but the dopeman. So what's the deal?"

Sean looked straight ahead. He might as well tell the truth.

"No, we don't live here, Darryl. But you're right. The dopeman does, and he's my brother."

Darryl grimaced.

"I'm using his address so I can go to Hamilton High. Hopefully, I can move in with him soon, even though my mom doesn't want me to actually live here."

"Hey lil' brother. You don't have to front for me. I'm from the 'hood, too. And, believe me, you're not the only one going to Hamilton High who doesn't live in the area. So as far as moving in with your brother, that's your business. I don't know if that's the best answer to your problem, but you be real careful moving around that house."

"Yeah I know, Darryl. But I'm clean. I don't have any interest in that stuff."

"You're on the right track kid. Take care. I've got pizza calling my name."

Sean went to the front door and rang the doorbell. He heard Jesse taking the locks off. He knew Jesse would be mad about him stopping by without asking or letting him know he was coming, but Sean did want to talk to Jesse about moving in with him. Jesse had told him before that it was O.K. with him, but they would need a plan to convince their mother.

Sean told Jesse about making the team and about Kevin's family. When he mentioned Darryl's name, Jesse grunted a recognition of the name. Then they discussed Sean's problem with commuting. Jesse told Sean he could move in whenever he was ready. Later, he drove Sean home and agreed to stay so they could try to convince their mother to let Sean make the move.

Sean and Jesse looked into each other's eyes. A siren screamed down a nearby street, and two teenaged girls argued loudly over a pair of earrings. Sean heard nothing. He had his hand on the doorknob, and he knew there was no turning back. Jesse had agreed to come with Sean to the house while he asked their mother for permission to move in with Jesse. They both knew how she felt about Jesse's lifestyle. Her disapproval of his drug dealings was strong and consistent. Sean took a deep, nervous breath and turned the doorknob. Neither of them noticed their mother, Louise, peering out of the curtain.

"Mama."

"You're late again, Sean."

"I know, Mama, but..."

"But nothing! Boy, where have you been? You know how I worry when you're late."

"Yeah I know, Mama, but I missed the bus. Jesse is here. He brought me home."

Both of them stepped into the living room and took off their hats. Louise faced them with her hands on her hips. She gave Jesse a long hard look.

"What happened? Did they repossess your mansion?"

"No, Mama, Sean asked me to come in, or else you know I wouldn't be here. Don't worry, I won't be stayin' long."

Bernice, a friend who had been talking to Louise, stood, slipped into her jacket, and began moving toward the door.

"Well, Lou, I think it's time for me to move on. You boys keep outta trouble. And if you'll just ease on over a bit, I'll be outta your conversation."

"Alright Bernice, I'll catch up with you later."

Louise straightened her apron.

"Why don't one of you close my door, and both of you find someplace to sit down. Meanwhile, I'll warm your dinner Sean."

Jesse sat on the sagging couch he had grown up with. He looked around the apartment and noticed how everything still looked the same. The furniture was all in the same place as it had been years ago. The carpet was worn, and the T.V. still had a hanger in place of the antenna. His eyes focused on a small burned spot. Jesse smiled to himself as the memory came back. That burn was from the time Mama had come home early, and caught Jesse and a friend trying to smoke cigarettes. ("Boy did we catch it that day.") The thought faded, and Jesse turned to Sean, who was seated across from him in their mother's favorite chair.

"I see nothing has changed around here."

"Hey, it's home man, and it used to be good enough for you."

"Yeah bro, that's the key word, 'used' to be good enough. So when you gonna pop the question so I can get out of here?"

"It's your house man, I thought you'd ask."

Jesse chuckled and shook his head.

"No buddy, this is your baby. Either you deal with it, or you stay here."

Sean looked at Jesse and smiled. He knew he'd have to ask, but he thought it was worth a try to see if Jesse would do it for him.

"Jesse, Mom doesn't want to cut the strings. You know how long it takes for me to get back and forth to school from here. It's a two-hour bus ride each way. If the school finds out, they'll put me out, and that's it for track, college, everything!"

"Yeah, and don't forget that pretty young thing called Denise."

Sean grinned.

"She counts too, but Mama wouldn't understand that part."

Louise came into the room with Sean's dinner, put it down in front of him and looked at both of them.

"Mama wouldn't understand that part of what?" she asked.

"Well, Jesse said I could stay with him, rather than keep traveling back and forth on the bus every day."

Louise turned to look at Jesse, and Jesse looked back.

"Oh, Jesse said so, huh? And what else did Jesse say?" Louise asked, still eyeing Jesse.

"Mama, it would be so much easier if I lived with Jesse."

"Boy, you must have run around that track one time too many. I think you have truly lost your mind. You are not staying out there with him."

Jesse stood up, reached for his hat and moved toward the door.

"Look, I already told Sean it was between you and him. My offer stands, so whatever y'all decide is cool with me. Just give me a call and let me know, but I have other things I need to be doing."

Louise stood and looked Jesse up and down.

"Yeah, well just make sure eating is one of those things. You look like you've lost weight, you're probably not eating right."

"Don't worry. I'm okay, and I'm eating just fine."

"Well, take care of yourself, son."

"Always do, Mama. Later."

Louise watches Jesse walk down the steps, closes the door and turns to Sean.

"You're not eating either, Sean. Eat your dinner."

"Mama, would you at least think about it? I'm spending four hours a day on the bus. If the school finds out where I live, that will be the end of my track career and any hopes for a college scholarship. This is like one of those obstacles you're always telling me about. We've already got enough obstacles, and if I have to keep going through all these changes every day, I'm not going to make it. I might as well just go to school down here."

"Oh Sean, is it that bad living here with me?"

"No, that's not what I'm saying, Mama. You know I love you, and I want to live with you, and I want you to be proud of me. But in order for me to make it at Hamilton, I need to live in the suburbs with Jesse. It has to be one or the other, Mama. I'm starting to feel like a secret agent with two identities. I can't keep it up for a whole year. It's up to you, it's your decision."

"Well, at least you got that part right. It is my decision just like all the other ones I've had to make for you all these years. You let me make the decisions around here, and you just take that plate in the kitchen and wash it, if you're finished with it."

Sean stood and picked up his plate. He put the last piece of cornbread in his mouth and headed for the kitchen. At the doorway he turned back to his mother.

"I'm not a fool, Mama. I don't think like Jesse, and I'm not going to be like him, either. You raised me right, Mama. I'm not going to forget that, even if I'm living away from home."

"But Jesse is 'pure street' baby. He is barely taking care of himself. He is so busy living in the fast lane. How is he going to take care of you? I'd be worried sick wondering if you were eating right and dressing properly. How are you going to study with his fancy friends coming and going all the time?"

Still holding the dishes, Sean took a few steps toward his mother. He had to try to make her understand.

"Those are things we can work out as we go along. I could come home every weekend and call you every night, or something. Can't we give it a try? If it doesn't work out, I'll come back here and that will be the end of it. I'll never ask you about it again."

Louise held her hands up, signaling Sean to stop.

"O.K. Sean, that's enough. Wash your dishes and hit the sack."

When Sean got to his room, he kicked off his sneakers, pulled off his Hamilton High sweatshirt, and sat on the edge of his bed with his head in his hands. He looked at the side of the room that used to belong to Jesse, and remembered the nights they used to lay in bed whispering, long after Mama thought they were sleep. He'd had some good times in this place, and some good times with Jesse, but he knew this was a time of change for him, and in his relationship with his brother. No matter what his mother's decision, nothing would be the same for him. He was seeing a whole new side of life, and while it was exciting, it was also scary. If only Mama could understand. There was a soft tap on his door. Sean looked up.

"Yes, Mama? Come on in."

Louise poked her head around the door.

"I just have one more question for you, Sean."

"What's that?"

"Who is Denise?"

"Denise. Who told you about Denise?"

"You did, baby."

Louise winked at Sean and smiled.

"Hey! You were listening to our conversation!"

"So who is she, this pretty young thing?"

Sean was smiling now. He rolled his eyes and wiggled his eyebrows.

"She's a girl I met at school. That's all. It's no big deal."

"Oh, I can understand that."

She imitated his actions with his eyebrows, gave him a thumbs-up and closed the door.

"Goodnight, Sean." she whispered.

"Goodnight, Mama."

Louise went into her bedroom and lets out a sigh. Her nightstand was covered with framed pictures of her boys from age one. Her favorite was the one of Sean and Jesse at the lake. They were in their swimming trunks and profiling like muscle builders. That had been the first time that day that there hadn't been a herd of young girls around them, so she had snapped the picture while she could. She took a picture of Sean in his running suit from her nightstand and held it close. She knew she had to make a decision about Sean, and she had to make it tonight.

By the time Sean was up and ready for school the next day, Louise had breakfast ready. Sean was moving slow and felt like just grabbing the juice and running out the door, but he knew his mother would never let that happen. He pulled his chair out and sat down.

"What's up, Mama? You've got enough food on this plate to feed a linebacker."

"Well pretend like it's your last real meal, because considering where you're going, it probably will be."

Louise nodded towards the front door where she had

packed some of Sean's belongings in a suitcase. Sean followed her gaze, dropped his toast, and leaped towards his mother. He grabbed her around the waist and whirled her around.

"Boy, put me down! See, you've gone nuts already!"

Sean stopped and held his mother's hands. He was so excited he could hardly talk.

"Ah, Mama, thank you, thank you. This is one decision you won't regret. This will make such a big difference. This is the best, the best thing you could have done for me!"

"Well I'm glad you think so, because I had my doubts. Now Sean, I'm gonna trust that you will do the right thing. Don't let me down."

Sean and Louise looked each other in the eyes, and time froze for a moment. They both knew the importance of the arrangement, and the trust that went with it. Louise hugged her son tightly and Sean hugged her back.

"Don't worry, Mama, you'll see, it's gonna work. I'll see to that."

"I know you will, baby. I know you will. I also know you just missed out on your last meal, because if you don't get out of here, you're going to miss your bus."

Sean looked at his watch.

"Oh no, I don't believe it!"

"I do, and I believe I'll just help myself to your breakfast too! You get going and I'll call Jesse and have him stop by to pick up your bag".

"O.K., Mama. Thanks."

Sean slid out the door and started toward the bus stop. As soon as he hit the sidewalk, the bus drove past him. Sean was so happy, it didn't bother him at all. He threw his bookbag on his back and took off running. He ran a block and caught the bus. As he dropped his bus fare in the coinbox, he looked at Roy, the driver, and laughed.

"Man, you gonna have to get some turbo in this slow bucket to beat me."

Roy waved him on.

"Yeah and you're going to have to get yourself some 'get

up out the bed turbo' if you're planning to catch this bus every morning. Next time I'm not going to slow down so you can catch me."

"Get real," Sean laughed. "Besides, this is the last time I'll be doing this, except for Mondays."

"How do you figure that? Did they put you out of school already?"

"No man, I'm moving in with my brother Jesse."

Roy had known Sean and his brother since they were young, and he knew all about Jesse's doings. He looked at Sean and grunted. He knew if Louise was allowing it, there had to be a good reason. So he left it alone and turned his attention to the young lady getting on the bus.

"O.K. lil' Jesse Owens, sit down somewhere, you're blocking my action. Well good morning, you must be a model or something, I saved a seat right up front for you."

Sean sat down and smiled to himself. He was feeling on top of the world. Things were happening fast, and they were going his way. He had that same special feeling he had whenever he ran. It was a really good feeling from the inside. It was what he called his "natural high." He usually felt it after participating in a track meet, but this was just as important to him, and felt just as good.

"Yo, Sean, wait up!" Kevin yelled.

"Hey Kevin, what's up?"

"Nothing much, man. Did you finish Coach's assignment?"

"Yeah, I had to do that one. I made sure when he asked about the Alps, that I mentioned that not only did Hannibal cross the Alps and conquer Rome, but that he was a black man."

"You know that's right! Give me five on that. So what else did you do last night?"

"I worked on my homework, and that's about it."

"I'm not talking about workin' on homework. I want to know if you worked on Denise!"

"Oh yeah, I walked her home yesterday."

"That I know. Now tell me what happened that I don't know about. Did you meet her folks? Or wouldn't they let you in the door!"

"Aw, man, that's cold-blooded. Her folks weren't even home when we got there."

"Whew! Yesss, break it down easy to me!. How was it?"

"Nice man, real nice."

"That's a dream come true man. A chick like Denise, and when you got there her parents weren't home. What a party!"

"Easy, wild man, I didn't go in the house. I kissed her at the front door and made sure she got in alright. Then I went home."

"Say what?" Kevin froze in his tracks, dropped his jaw and stared at Sean in disbelief.

"Did I hear you say you kissed her and went home? You must need some serious therapy, boy. I mean some serious, long term kind of help. Nobody in their right mind would do a thing like that."

"No," Coach interrupted. "Only somebody in their right mind would do a thing like that."

The boys had been so involved in their conversation that they hadn't noticed that the coach was walking right behind them.

"Kevin, Sean just got here, don't start corrupting him already."

"No sir, I wouldn't think of it." Kevin replied.

They had reached the doorway of the classroom and Coach nudged them inside.

"Good, because I would hate to see any of your bad habits starting to rub off."

They all laughed and took their places.

"Take out your homework from last night," Coach told the class.

Kevin and Sean looked at each other. Kevin was still shaking his head in disbelief. Sean smiled and held up his homework. Kevin smiled back, then turned his attention towards the coach.

The next afternoon after practice, Kevin and Sean were heading toward the locker room. Kevin noticed J.R. quickly moving in on them.

"Oh, oh, here comes the number one pain in the butt."

Sean looked over his shoulder just as J.R. reached them.

"Say Sean, if you just moved in this area, why did I see you getting off a bus a few days ago? It seems a little strange for you to have to take a public bus to the corner up there, and then have to run the rest of the way. I was expecting to see a police car pull up behind you."

Kevin put his hands on his hips and stepped in front of J.R.

"You know, J.R., everything seems strange to you, and what could be more strange than what you see in your mirror every morning? Or have you broken all of them already?"

"Look, don't get in my face with that stuff, Kevin. And if I hear about you hanging out with my sister again, you're going to be real familiar with the word strange. Especially after I wrap your legs around your neck."

"My legs and Lisa's arms around my neck. It's going to be tough but, we'll manage"

J.R. started at Kevin.

"That's it, man. Meet me after school."

"Sorry, Lisa's got me booked for the evening."

J.R. mumbled under his breath and stormed away. Sean turned to Kevin and slapped him on the back.

"Well done, my brother. Now do you know where I can find a J.O.B.?"

"That shouldn't be a problem, man. Check out the malls, they usually have signs all over the place."

"Cool, I'll just call my brother and let him know where I'll be."

"You don't have to do it today you know. Why don't you hang out at my place for a while?"

"Yeah, you're right. I think I will. Your dad wanted to talk anyway. I'll call Jesse from your house."

Sean was browsing through Darryl's book collection, while Darryl and Kevin listened to a tape of his group's reggae music. Darryl had been into Bob Marley and reggae music from Jamaica for years. Sean came across a book by Dr.

Jawanza Kunjufu, titled "Countering the Conspiracy to Destroy Black Boys".

"Whoa, what is this about?" Sean said out loud.

"What's up youngblood?" Darryl asked.

Sean took the book off of the shelf. He turned it around towards Darryl and Kevin.

"What is 'Countering the Conspiracy' to Destroy Black Boys?"

Darryl smiled. "The book is about a conspiracy in America to rob young brothers of their manhood, dignity and lives. It will take you back to the fourth grade, and show you how the system has and will, play with your mind like a yo-yo."

Darryl shook his dreadlocks and pointed to The Autobiography of Malcolm X.

"You think the info on Hannibal was heavy. Man, check out the truth about Beethoven and Moses and...

There's a lot of information that can't be found in your history book that really is history, or maybe I should say it's 'our-story.' Believe me, when race isn't mentioned, there's usually a good reason for the omission."

Mr. Wilkes thought he heard voices in the basement and moved to the top of the stairs. He heard Sean's voice and smiled to himself. He was impressed with Kevin's new friend and wanted to get to know him better. He reminded him of lot of himself when he was coming up.

"Hey Kevin, Sean, come on up. How's the track coming along?"

Kevin motioned for Sean to go on upstairs.

"Go on up, Sean. He really wants to talk to you."

"Well you come with me. He called both of us you know."

"Yeah, but you're the one with the Olympic potential. That's what turns him on."

Sean climbed the paneled staircase to the den. He stopped as he stepped on the luxurious, ivory-colored carpet. He slid his feet out of his sneakers and walked into the room. The walls were covered with African masks, paintings and papyrus prints. The plants in the room were so large and green that they looked artificial. Mr. Wilkes was seated on a chocolate brown leather couch ,with a stack of thick books in front of him. As Sean got closer, he realized that they weren't books, but photo albums.

"What's in the albums?" Sean asked.

Mr. Wilkes patted the space on the couch next to him.

"Here, have a seat. I've got some old photos of when I used to be a track star myself. No one else around here appreciates seeing these anymore. Kevin just doesn't seem to be interested, but I thought you might."

"Sure, I'd like to check them out."

Sean sat down next to Mr. Wilkes. They spent the next two hours talking about track, Mr. Wilkes' records, and Sean's potential. Sean decided he enjoyed spending time with Mr. Wilkes and hoped he would be able to do it more often. But it was getting late, and he was afraid Jesse would be worried. He knew Mama would call if he didn't call soon.

"Mr. Wilkes these are some great photos, but, I'd better be getting home now."

"The time has passed quickly, Sean. I'm glad you enjoyed the pictures. Maybe we can get together more often."

Sean put his hand out towards Mr. Wilkes and they shook hands.

"You can count on that Mr. Wilkes."

"Good. Let me give you a lift home."

Sean and Mr. Wilkes drove in silence for a while. Then Mr. Wilkes asked Sean about his father.

"Sean, I hear you mentioning your mother and your brother, but you've never mentioned your father. Is there a reason for that?"

"My father died when I was young, Mr. Wilkes. Unfortunately I never got to know him."

Mr. Wilkes turned to look at Sean.

"Oh, I'm sorry to hear that, Sean."

"It's O.K. I couldn't have asked for a better mother. Mama is the best."

"Yeah, I can tell you love her a lot. And she has done a great job raising you, too."

"Thanks."

The car pulled up in front of Jesse's house and Sean got out. He closed the car door, and leaned in the window.

"Thanks for everything Mr. Wilkes."

"Oh, you're welcome, Sean. Anytime."

Mr. Wilkes smiled and pulled off. Sean went around to the back door, opened the screen door, and tried the doorknob. The door was locked, so he rang the doorbell. Suddenly the door swung open, and Sean found himself looking down the double barrel of a shotgun. He froze with his mouth hanging open and his eyes bulging.

"Cheez-n-bread, man! I almost erased your face, fool. What do you think you're doing?"

Jesse lowered the gun and grabbed Sean by the shoulder with his free hand. He jerked him inside and slammed the door shut. Sean was staring at the shotgun.

"Man, I wasn't doing anything. What are you doing? Is that the way you answer the doorbell?"

Jesse went into the living room. He stopped on his way to put the gun in the hall closet.

"Look, birdbrain. I told you to call before you come home, so I can be on the lookout for you. If you can't handle a simple rule like that you'd better head back down to Mama's."

"Sorry, I forgot."

"Naw, brother, it's not about that sorry stuff. 'Cause once I blow your head off, you won't be able to hear my apology. Either you call before you come, or you don't come. Got it?"

"Yes Jesse, I got it."

"Cool."

Jesse sat down in his soft leather recliner, and reached for his drink and his earphones. Sean admired his clothes and the way they fit Jesse's muscular body.

"Like your outfit, Jesse."

"I'm sure you do, and I hope you like the ones I bought and put in your closet. You really don't have much choice though, since I threw out those rags you brought with you. No brother of mine is going to be seen looking like some jack-in -the -box clown, coming in and out of my house."

Sean broke out in a grin.

"Thanks, Jesse. You're alright."

"Yeah, now do you have any cash to put in your pockets?"

"Not really, but it's cool. I'm going to try to get a job at the mall tomorrow."

"A job at the mall? What are you planning on doing? Washing out garbage cans or something? Nobody is going to give you a job. You can't do anything. Plus you've got to concentrate on track and school, not to mention that little fox you've been hunting."

"Well, I'm talking about something part-time, Jesse. Maybe a couple of hours a day."

"It'll never happen my man. But, I might be able to hook you up with a little something you can do for about an hour each week. You can have plenty of cash and time to spend on your little sweet thing, and take care of your books too!"

"It doesn't sound real, Jesse. Or maybe I should say, 'it doesn't sound legal.'"

Sean turned and headed toward the spiral staircase.

"Suit yourself, kid. And call Mama before you hit the sack."

Jesse put on his earphones and sat back in his recliner. Sean went upstairs and closed his bedroom door. He called his mother and let her know how things were going. Then he decided to call Denise. The only problem was what he would say. Would she want to talk? He took a chance and dialed her number.

The phone rang. Sean became tense and held his breath. It rang again. On the fourth ring, her answering machine took the call. Sean hung up the phone without leaving a message.

"Hmm, maybe it's just as well. I'll need a job before I could date Denise seriously. I might as well go to bed."

Sean picked up his shoes and walked to the closet. As he opened the door, his new wardrobe surprised him.

"Whew, look at this stuff! I'll knock 'em dead with one look."

Sean took out a shirt, one in each hand. He held one up to his chest and then the other. He chose an outfit for the next day, and hung it up separately. He closed his mirrored closet doors, and went into the adjoining bathroom.

Sean wasn't used to such luxury, but he was beginning to enjoy it. He got undressed, turned on the hot water in the bathtub, and relaxed. His mind flashed briefly to Jesse pulling the shotgun on him this afternoon. He had heard of similar situations in the projects, and even seen some people who had been shot or hurt in gang wars. But, he had never had a gun pulled on him. He wondered how Jesse maintained himself living on the edge like that all the time. Sean knew it was Jesse's way of doing things, and that he would have to steer clear of his schemes.

After his bath he dried off and put on his new silk pajamas Jesse had given him. He got into the bed, turned off the lights and thought about tomorrow's track practice. As his mind wandered he thought about Denise, and how he could impress her. Then he noticed how different it was sleeping at Jesse's house. The major difference was the silence. There were no fights, no cursing, no gunfire, and rarely a siren. It was certainly different from home in the projects, but with what Jesse and some of the other suicidal suburbanites went through to keep it, Sean wondered if it was really better.

The next day after track practice, Sean and Kevin were sitting on a bench in the locker room, going over some of the coach's strategies. Practice had been very good, especially for Sean.

"Sean, if you run in the next meet, the way you ran today, you'll have first place hands down."

"Yeah, you know it felt. . ."

"Felt what? Felt kind of crowded in the winner's circle to me boys."

J.R. had moved around to where Sean and Kevin were sitting. Sean had bumped him out of a first place finish during practice and J.R. was not happy about it.

"I wouldn't let it go to my head though, it'll never happen again. And never in a real meet, so enjoy it while you can."

J.R. started walking away. Sean and Kevin looked at each other and shook their heads.

"He's going to be real upset when we dust him in the meet won't he?"

Kevin laughed. "You know that's right!

As the boys were headed out of the locker room, Kevin invited Sean over for dinner.

"You know I love your mother's cooking, but I'm going to the mall to see if I can get a part time job. Do you want to hang?"

"Naw, I'll get one during the summer. My mother hits the ceiling every time I mention working during the school year."

"Well, I'll never make it without some money from somewhere, so I'm off."

J.R. had been standing behind a row of lockers, listening to the conversation. He had worked at the mall for a couple of years, and knew almost all the managers by name. He'd make sure that none of them hired Sean.

The next day in the hallway, Sean was telling Kevin how strange some of the store managers had acted when he asked about a job.

"Two of them did let me fill out an application and promised to call last night, but only one called, and that was to tell me that I hadn't been hired. I didn't think it would be this hard." Sean said frustrated.

"Hey Sean! Sean! "It was J.R. and his buddies coming down the corridor.

"How did the job hunting go? Any luck?"

Sean looked at J.R. and then Kevin. How did J.R. know he was in the market for a job? Kevin shrugged his shoulders. He wondered the same thing.

"Not so good man, what's it to you?, "Kevin replied.

"So this is the thanks I get? I put in my own special recommendations for you, and look at the thanks I get."

J.R. slapped one of his sidekicks on the back and they all burst out laughing.

"Well, give my mom a call Sean, she could use some help with the housework. I may even recommend you to her too!"

They laughed again and ran off down the hall.

"I think maybe I know why you had such a hard time with the job hunting." Kevin said.

"Yeah, it's hard to believe, but I think I can thank J.R. for not being hired by anybody."

The bell rang and they took off running for class.

"Don't worry, something will come up for you." Kevin whispered as he grabbed the doorknob to his English class.

"Yeah, I'm sure." Kevin had to run upstairs to his class. He hoped Mrs. Carson hadn't started yet.

Later that evening, while Jesse was cooking dinner, Sean told him about his job hunting experience. Jesse kept shaking his head while he served the meal on their plates.

"O.K., I know, you told me not to bother. But I had to find out for myself, and know that at least I tried."

"Yeah, and you can see where that got you, man."

"I know. The worst part is that I wanted to ask Denise to the big dance coming up. I really wanted to do it up. You know with dinner first at The Seafood House, and then head over to the dance afterwards." Sean pushed his food around on his plate with a glum expression on his face. Jesse looked at him, and appeared to be thinking.

"Hey, don't look so down. I've got an idea. Why don't you work for me?"

Sean looked at him and rolled his eyes.

"Get real, Jesse. I'm going to college, not to jail."

"Don't dis' me man. If you were in jail, then you couldn't be working for me, now could you? I'm talking about some simple stuff, man. Laundry, washing my cars, maybe some shopping sometimes. Do you think they will lock you up for that? Or aren't you interested?"

Sean sat up and looked at Jesse. " Laundry and errands, is that it?"

"Yeah, that's it. Especially the laundry. There's nothing I hate more than doing laundry."

"Well, you don't do it anyway. You drop it off over on the Avenue."

"It's still something that has to be done, and I don't like

doing it."

"Cool man, I'll work for you. As long as it's legitimate, I'm game."

"Deal, you can start tonight with these dishes, and I'll pack the laundry in a bag and leave it over in the corner by the broomcloset. Just take it over to the place on the Avenue, give it to Brent, and tell him you're dropping it off for me. Not too much to do for a hundred bucks a week is it?"

"Consider it done, Jesse! Thanks man. You don't know how much I appreciate you helping me out like this."

"No problem, blood. You're helping me out, too."

Sean was feeling good now. He finished up his dinner and washed the dishes.

"Hey, Jesse, I'll be back in a little while. Denise is going to give me some dancing lessons at her house."

"Fine, but I'm not paying for no dancing lessons, brother."

"Very funny. Bye!" Sean left out the front door. Jesse watched him walk down the driveway. Then Jesse called to tell the others he worked with about his new idea.

As the days passed, Sean and Denise become closer in their friendship. Sean was content. He had a job, his track, and Denise and Kevin.

However, Denise was becoming a little restless. She and Lisa were sitting on Lisa's bed with shopping bags scattered around them. Denise reached in a bag and pulled out a short silk dress.

"Now if this dress, and my new haircut don't get Sean in the mood, nothing will! Lisa I have tried everything I can think of to get Sean to be more romantic. But all he does is kiss me goodnight, and I have to almost wrestle him in a corner to get that. I mean even at the movies, he just sits there with his arm around me."

"Did it ever occur to you that maybe he wants to actually see the movie, Denise?"

Denise dropped back on the bed pretending to pull out her hair. "Oh heaven help me. I'm surrounded by deadbeats. What's a girl to do?" she croaked.

They laughed. Denise jumped off of the bed. "Tonight,

tonight will be different. I asked Sean over and we'll have the whole place to ourselves."

"You act like that's the first time that has happened. So what."

"This time, it will be different. She held her dress up to her and threw her head back. This silk dress is on my side tonight."

"Yeah, it barely covers your sides." It was Lisa's turn to fall back on the pillow. Oh heaven help her. She doesn't understand the man has other things on his mind." Denise picked up another pillow and threw it in Lisa's face. "Be quiet, you're jinxing my night." She put her dress back in the bag, and took out a bottle of cologne. " And now the secret weapon!" she smiled at Lisa and winked. Lisa shook her head and held her wrist out so Denise could let her test it.

"Mmm, it does smell good."

"Hey you don't have to tell me that. Why do you think I bought it?"

"Because you think Sean will fall for it."

"Yep, you got it!"

Lisa thought for a moment. "Don't forget there's a track meet tomorrow."

"The track meet doesn't have anything on what I've got planned."

"Well, try to tell Sean that."

Denise looked at Lisa."If he comes up with that line again, girl, the party is over. And I mean over."

The girls talked a little longer. Then Denise helped clean up the mess and headed home. She was excited and couldn't wait for Sean to come over.

Denise opened the door for Sean. She was wearing her "secret weapon," her new dress, and her sexiest smile. Behind her, the CD player was putting out some soft, soulful sounds. Sean took one look at Denise and froze.

"Whew-ee-baby!" Sean's eyes grew wider.

"Hi, Sean. Come on in."

"Just let me stand here a minute and take in the scenery!"

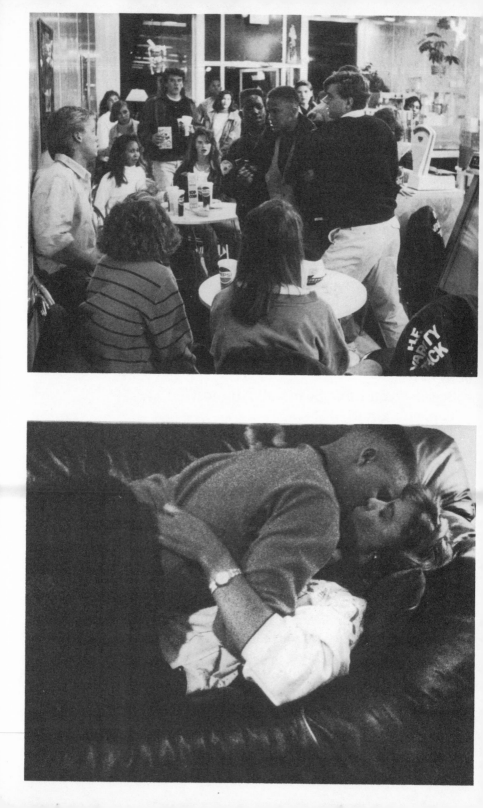

Denise smiled. This was the reaction she had hoped for. "Let's go downstairs in the rec room."

"Sweetheart, I will follow you anywhere." Sean was mesmerized by her appearance. Denise smiled and they went downstairs.

The basement was half-marbled and half-carpeted. There was an entertainment center on one wall with a 46" television and stereo system. There was also an extensive library shelved on one wall. The carpet was a deep royal blue. The couch was ivory colored, and the paneling was a peach print. Denise had strategically turned two lamps on low. There were two man-sized African statues, and one large Dali print to accent the room. Sean looked around in awe. It was nothing like he had seen before.

"Wow! Who lives down here?"

"Who lives down here? Nobody lives down here. This is the basement. It's our family room."

Sean glanced in the open doorway to the left.

"What do you mean family room. A family room with a kitchen?"

Denise giggled. "That's not a kitchen silly, that's a bar. The microwave is for heating up snacks. Hey, that's the end of the tour. I thought you came to see me." Denise pouted and crossed her arms. Sean hugged her and kissed her on both cheeks.

"Yeah, you're right. I didn't come for a tour anyway. But I'm not sure I'll be able to concentrate on my dance lessons when the teacher looks and smells so good." Sean rocked Denise back and forth, and she put her arms around his neck.

"Well, if we keep the music slow enough, we won't have to worry about any lessons," Denise whispered in Sean's ear. Sean took her hands down from around his neck.

"Let's not get too carried away, now.I don't want you to back out on your promise to teach me how to dance."

Denise kissed him lightly on the lips. "I said I'd teach you how to dance, so I'm going to start with slow dance. Do you have any complaints?"

Sean sighed. "How can I complain about spending time with you?"

Denise took Sean by the hand and led him to the largest of the three couches. She sat back, and pulled his arms around her waist."

"What are you doing Denise?" Sean kissed her on the neck and pulled away.

"Nothing Sean, nothing." Denise got up and changed the music.

"Do you want a soda?"

Sean watched her move across the room. Her legs were perfect and her skin was glowing under her short dress.

"Actually, a glass of ice water would be fine." Sean replied. Denise rolled her eyes and got some water for Sean and a soft drink for herself.

She showed him a few steps to some upbeat music. They danced for about a half an hour, and then she flopped down on the couch.

"O.K. Sean, it's time for a break."

"Yeah, you're right." He flopped down next to her, and laid his head on her shoulder. "Girl, you sure know how to wear a guy out. You can really move." Denise pushed Sean off her shoulder, and sat on his lap. She unbuttoned his shirt, and kissed him on the neck.

"Sean I'm really glad you came over today." Denise took his hand and rested it on her thigh. They looked each other in the eye and leaned toward each other for a kiss. Sean's hand eased up her thigh and under her dress. She put her hands behind his neck and gently pressed her lips against his. His other hand slowly moved up her side and slightly brushed across her breast, and around her back. Denise unbuttoned the next two buttons on his shirt, and rubbed her hand across his chest. Sean felt himself growing excited and pulled away. Denise was surprised.

"Uh, Denise, I think I'd better be going." Sean was breathing deeply.

"What's the matter Sean? Don't you want to be with me?"

"I'd like to, but, I don't think we're ready yet."

"What do you mean? I'm ready, and from what I can see, you're ready too."

"No, Denise, I'm not ready. And neither are you. We'd be taking a risk by going all the way now." Sean reached for his water.

"Risk? I'm not taking any risk." Denise reached behind Sean and brought out a pack of condoms from the end table. When she stretched, her dress rose even higher, and her lace panties showed for a brief moment. Sean could feel his temperature rising and stood up.

"No Denise, that's not the answer. And this isn't the place."

Denise looked around. "Well if you want, we can go upstairs to my room. My parents won't be back until tomorrow. Come on Sean, don't be a drag. We were just starting to warm up."

Denise stood up and tried to put her arms around Sean. Sean caught her wrist in mid-air and held them by her sides.

"No, Denise. I think I'd better leave."

Denise was beginning to get aggravated. It was usually some boy chasing after her. She could think of plenty of people who would be happy to spend an evening alone with her.

"Yeah, Sean, maybe you'd better go. I think you may need a lot more lessons than I'm willing to give." Denise stormed across the room and took Sean's coat out of the closet. She tossed it at him and headed towards the stairs. Sean followed.

"Look Denise, I didn't mean any offense," he started.

Denise yanked the door open and put her other hand on her hip. "Oh Sean, believe me, none was taken. Just get the hell out of my house and don't waste any more of my time." Sean put his coat on and left. Denise slammed the door and started to cry. No one had ever made her feel so rejected.

As Lisa and Kevin walked into the schoolyard, they were surprised to see J.R. leaning on his car, with his arm around Denise's shoulder.

"For some reason, that picture doesn't seem quite right does it, Lisa?"

They slowed down as they got closer to the car. "You're right, Kevin. What is my brother doing with his arm around her? Where's Sean?"

"I haven't seen him since yesterday during practice."

"Well, I know they were supposed to get together last night. But this shouldn't be the result of that. Not according to the plans Denise had made."

" I guess things didn't go according to plan, huh?" Kevin walked up to J.R. and Denise. " This looks cozy. What's happening Denise? Where's Sean?"

"Kevin, do I look like Sean's babysitter? I couldn't care less where that track rat is hiding. Come on J.R., it's getting crowded out here."

"Yeah, you're right. Let's go."

Denise and J.R. walked towards the building. Lisa and Kevin looked at each other, and slowly followed. Sean met J.R. and Denise at the door.

"Denise. I've been looking all over for you. What are you doing walking around with your arms around him?" Sean cocked his head towards J.R.. Denise rested her head on J.R.'s shoulder. "I guess I needed a man's shoulder to lean on Sean."

"And, since you don't fit that description, I'm taking up the slack for you," J.R. sneered. Sean ignored J.R.

"Denise, can we talk?"

"I'm tired of talking, Sean. I've got to get to class. See ya at lunch, J.R.?"

" Yeah, later."

Denise went upstairs, and J.R. headed towards the basement.

"Hey J.R., this isn't over you know."

"I know man, I'm just getting started." he laughed and kept walking. Kevin and Lisa came in one door, as Sean kicked another.

"Easy bro', the day is just beginning. What's going on?" Kevin asked.

"Man, it's Denise." He looked at Lisa. "What is she trying to prove Lisa?"

"Look, I just got here too. She was fine when she left my house last night. You tell me what the deal is."

The first period bell rang. "It's a long story, but it's not worth this J.R. stuff. I'll catch you guys later." Sean ran up the stairs two at a time, and Lisa and Kevin both quickly headed to class, wondering what they had missed.

Later that morning, Kevin went to the locker room to switch his track shoes. He had decided to save his new shoes for a meet coming up later in the season. The shoes he had on were soft and already "broken in". As he came around the corner of a row of lockers, he saw J.R. popping something into his mouth, and slip a little vial into a pouch on his track bag. He looked the other way first, and was startled when he turned to see Kevin on his other side. He blushed and had a guilty look on his face.

"What are you looking at, Kevin? Can't a person take their vitamins in private?"

"Locker rooms aren't known for their privacy, J.R., and why would you wait until lunchtime to take a vitamin?"

"Don't worry about why I do what I do, punk." J.R. slammed his locker, grabbed his bag, and left. Kevin watched him leave, and went to his locker to make the switch. He decided he didn't have time to be bothered with J.R. and whatever he was up to. He took off his red jacket, and put it in his locker and left.

It was during a study hall that Kevin remembered what he had seen J.R. do earlier in the day. A group of girls were sitting together talking about the boys in the room, and J.R.'s name came up during their conversation. One of the girls had commented on how muscular J.R. had become since last year. Someone said he probably worked out with weights, and one of the others mentioned that maybe he had taken something to help build up his muscles. That was when it hit Kevin what J.R. probably had been taking that morning. J.R. was using steroids. A dangerous risk for an athlete to take, just to make himself look good, or to set a record. Kevin stared at J.R.. One of J.R.'s friends noticed Kevin watching, and brought J.R.'s attention to it. J.R.

stared back momentarily, and then turned his back to Kevin. He motioned to two of his buddies to come closer.

"Hey guys listen up", J.R. whispered. "I've got a little problem, and it's sitting over at that table." He nodded to the table behind him where Kevin was sitting. "You know I've got to make a good showing in this meet today and the one on Saturday if I'm going to get that scholarship I'm after. Well, if something isn't done, that little wimp behind me may ruin it for me. Now, I need you guys to help me out." The boys agreed to help and moved closer to discuss what they could do. Shortly afterwards, the bell rang and the other students gathered their belongings and left. J.R. and his three buddies were still huddled together whispering.

After the track meet, Kevin and Ricardo were standing on the sidewalk talking. Ricardo was a friend of Kevin's since grade school. They were the same age and build, and even walked a lot alike. Ricardo, or "Rico" as most people called him, was impressed with Kevin's performance in the meet. "Man, you and Sean really put on a show today. Your posse dusted the rest of those guys. We've got to win the division on Saturday, with you two, there's no doubt about our chances."

"Thanks Rico. Coming from you, that means a lot. You know, if you had tried out, you'd be dusting us! I'll never forget the way you chewed up that track on the junior varsity team."

"Yeah, those were the days, my man. I don't have the time this year. Are you headed home? If you are, I'll walk with you."

"Naw man, I'm going to take the bus, and pick up a sweatsuit I put in layaway at the mall. Here, you'd better take my jacket though, the temperature is dropping, and a long walk seems even longer when it's cold." Kevin tossed Ricardo his red jacket.

"Thanks, man. I'll bring it tomorrow."

"Cool. Catch up with you later."

Kevin and Ricardo headed in different directions. As the

sun went down Ricardo put on the red jacket. He pulled the jacket collar up around his neck, and pulled his cap down low. A couple of blocks from the school, he noticed the sounds of footsteps behind him. He started to turn and see who it was, but he figured it was probably just some other students. As the footsteps got closer, he recognized two of the voices. Just as he was turning, he felt a stinging blow to his left leg, and then he felt himself being lifted off of the ground, and thrown into a tree trunk. His hat fell off as he slid into the grass. He heard his attackers cursing, and saying something about "the wrong one." The owner of the house came out on the porch yelling, and everyone ran, leaving Ricardo on the ground. She rushed to see if Ricardo was O.K.. He told her his back was sore and his leg was throbbing. She got his phone number and called his parents. They took him to the emergency ward at the hospital, where they told him he would be sore for a few days, and have difficulty walking, but that nothing was really damaged.

As Ricardo explained what had happened to his mother the second time, he realized that his attackers had mistaken him for Kevin, because of the red jacket. They were trying to hurt Kevin just enough to keep him from running on Saturday. He hoped Kevin would get home before it was too late to call him.

Meanwhile, Sean and Lisa were finishing their milkshakes at an ice cream store. They had been discussing Denise, as well as Sean's big plans for the school dance on Friday night. He had been trying to get Lisa to agree to convince Denise to keep their date and drop J.R. Lisa had agreed to try to get Denise to at least go to the dance, but she didn't know if she could help him with the date or J.R.

"Well just try Lisa. I'll owe you forever!"

"Look Sean, it's not going to be that easy. You know what Denise wants, and my brother will be more than happy to oblige her."

"Yeah I know Lisa, but she's got to want more out of life than sex and romance."

"Keep dreaming, Sean."

Sean looked at his watch. "Wow! It's way past seven! I was supposed to drop off my brother's laundry at 6:30. I've got to get out of here. Do you know of a laundromat that stays open late?"

"The one over on Main St. stays open until ten. But that's in the opposite direction of the one you go to on the Avenue."

"That's O.K. I just want to get it done so he won't have any excuse not to pay me Friday." They cleared their table and went outside. Lisa got into her car and offered Sean a ride and he accepted.

"Thanks Lisa, you saved me some time."

"Sure Sean, anytime. And I'll see what I can get out of Denise."

"Great. See you tomorrow!" Sean ran into the house and grabbed the laundry bag. He wanted to get Jesse's clothes done because he planned to give his mother a new outfit to wear to the track meet on Saturday. He decided he'd better sort the clothes first, and went to get another laundry bag. He dumped the clothes on the floor and began sorting them according to color. Light colored clothes in one pile, whites and dark ones in another. As he grabbed a handful of undershirts, something fell out of the bunch. It was a package of white powder wrapped several times in cellophane. He reached to pick it up, and suddenly a car screeched into the driveway and the car doors slammed. Jesse stormed into the house cursing. He stopped when he saw Sean and the laundry, and the package on the floor.

"You idiot!" Jesse yelled. "Give me that!"

"I could have been killed," Sean yelled back. "You would let your own brother be killed over some drugs. You don't care about anybody! Just money and drugs!

"Yo, little brother, I care about a lot of things. I care about my house, I care about my car, I even care about you. And since when do you still care? You look pretty good in those drug-money clothes, and you seem pretty comfortable in this drug-money mansion."

"Yeah, but for me, it's only temporary. I don't plan to grow up to be a junkie."

"Junkie?" Jesse laughed. I'm not stupid enough to use that stuff. I'm just smart enough to sell it because if I don't someone else will. And there's plenty of money to be made."

"That's disgusting."

Jesse grabbed the package and the phone in one smooth move. He told whoever was on the phone that he was on his way, slammed the receiver down and got back into the car. Sean could hear arguing, but the voices were muffled because the windows were up. The car pulled off, and Sean stood staring at the clothes on the floor. The phone rang again. This time Sean answered and it was Kevin.

"Hey, I hear they had a big-time drug bust at the laundry you use. Did you see or hear anything? Yo, Sean, are you there?"

"I'm here man. Who told you that?"

"My brother, Darryl. You know something about it? Darryl said they've been casing the place for a while now, and had expected to catch a drop at about six-thirty tonight. He told me to call you and see if you had heard about it."

"Tell him I didn't know. Is he there now?"

"Yeah, he's right here."

"Can you put him on the phone?"

Darryl got on the phone and questioned Sean about his laundry drops. Sean explained to him that he hadn't made it to the laundry on time, and didn't have any idea about what was going on until just a few minutes ago.

He assured Darryl that he wasn't part of the operation. He hung up the phone, stuffed the laundry back in the bag and left it on the floor. He went upstairs to his room.

Sean couldn't believe that Jesse had used him like that. He could be in jail right now because of Jesse. He also could have lost the best friends he ever had, if they thought he had anything to do with drugs. Sean decided to call his mother. He wouldn't tell her what had happened because it would just upset her. But he had convinced her to come to the house for dinner after the track meet on Saturday. Now, he didn't want her to be seen coming in the house. He wasn't sure he wanted to be seen either, since the police probably think he has something to do with Jesse and his friend's operation. Sean was upset. He didn't know what to do, so he decided to go to bed. He was restless. He heard the phone ring several times, but he didn't answer it.

The next morning, Sean woke up late, feeling tired. After he showered and dressed, he went downstairs. Everything was just like he left it. The lights were on, the radio was still playing, and Jesse was nowhere in sight. He was scared. Maybe he should have told Mama. Suppose something had happened to Jesse. What if whoever was supposed to get the drugs, took it out on Jesse and hurt him?

Sean went into the kitchen. The clothes were still on the floor in the bag. He looked around and saw five, twenty dollar bills on the table. That was how Jesse usually left his payment on Friday mornings. He always said he didn't want him running around flashing one hundred dollar bills. At least he knew Jesse was all right. Sean only took one of the bills, and left. He didn't want any part of drug money, and twenty was enough for the work he did each week. As he got to the corner of the street, Darryl and Kevin pulled up beside him.

"Hop in man. I think that's the first time I've ever seen you actually walk to school. At that speed, you'll barely get there in time for lunch." Darryl was smiling as he unlocked the car door behind him. Sean got in.

"Thanks Darryl. I guess I'm a little out of it today."

"Well, I guess so man, I could barely sleep myself, just thinking about you!" Kevin said. Darryl gave him a look.

"Yeah, sure, I could hear you snoring all the way downstairs. Barely sleep my foot." They laughed and finished the ride talking about the dance, and the track meet. Everyone knew Coach didn't like his runners partying the night before a meet, but tonight would have to be an exception for Sean and Kevin. Lisa had called and said that Denise would be going to the dance. The bad part is that she would be going with J.R.

Sean found it difficult to concentrate in school. Rico had told them about his incident with J.R.'s friends. Kevin was furious, but no one had seen J.R. or his buddies. Sean felt that things were getting worse and worse.

He wanted to tell Jesse to keep away from the laundry, since the police were watching and waiting for someone to make a move. He tried to reach Jesse on the pay phone at the school, but didn't have any luck. Then he decided he would go home during lunch and if Jesse wasn't there, he could ask Darryl to try to reach him.

When Sean got home he could tell Jesse had been home. The money and the laundry were gone. Sean called out. But there was no answer. He hoped Jesse hadn't gone to the laundry. He ran through the living room, and started up the stairs. Then he saw the laundry bag in the corner near the stairs. He lifted it up and looked inside. It wasn't the bag of laundry. There were at least ten packages like the one he had found the night before. Sean gasped. He took the bag into the kitchen, and took out two of the packages. He grabbed a knife and split the bags. He emptied the contents into the sink and turned the water on. He did the next two bags the same way. Then, he put the laundry bag into a brown paper bag and ran out of the house. He ran to the shopping center two blocks away and threw the bag in one of the large garbage dumpsters behind the stores. He looked at his watch, and knew he had to get back to school right away. He ran back to the house to get some clothes and toiletries, and headed back to school. He stopped at a pay phone and talked to Darryl, who agreed to try to warn Jesse. Sean was worried, and he had a bad feeling in his stomach. He knew there was nothing he could do, so he had to try to relax. He thought about the dance, and tried to figure out how he could win Denise back.

That evening, Sean dressed at Kevin's house. Kevin's parents had gone out to dinner, and there was no sign of Darryl. Both boys were a little down at first, but, as they showered and dressed, they put the incident with Rico and the problem with Jesse out of their minds. They had expected Darryl to drop them off at the dance, and since he wasn't home they decided to catch a ride with one of the other track team members.

There was a good turnout at the dance, and everyone was out to have a good time. Lisa was standing near the entrance, waiting on them.

"What took you guys so long? I knock myself out making sure Denise comes, and you drag in like it doesn't matter." Sean's face lit up.

"Where is she? Is she alone?"

"Sean, I told you she was coming with J.R., so that's who she's with."

"Aw crap! Why'd she do that?"

"Don't let that stop you, man. You can still ask her to dance." Kevin could see Sean was disappointed.

Sean looked at Lisa. Lisa started backing away, and shook her head.

"Lisa, you've got to help me. Just one more thing, and I promise I won't ask you for any more favors." Sean pretended like he was going to get down on one knee.

"No Sean. I'm going to get lost in the crowd, and enjoy myself."

"Great! Just do me this favor first. Get Denise away from J.R."

"Look at them. I think she has glued herself to him. How am I going to get her by herself?"

"I don't know, think of something."

I'll try, but not right now. Come on Kevin, let's dance." Kevin took Lisa's hand, headed for the dance floor and told her, "Remember, we're just friends, not lovers."

"Sure Kevin. Sean, you see if you can get us some seats. Preferably at a table."

"Yeah, alright." Sean looked around for some empty seats. As he scanned the room he saw J.R. and one of his cronies by the punch table. J.R. was busy watching Kevin and Lisa but, his friend spotted Sean and stared back. Then he smiled and waved. Sean nodded and continued to look in another direction. He spotted a table with two chairs, and decided he might as well save them for Kevin and Lisa. He got Kevin's attention and pointed to the table. Kevin gave him a thumbs up.

J.R. watched what was happening and smiled. He turned to Denise.

"Well, it looks like all the players are here. I'm surprised they're out the night before a meet."

"I'm with the only person I want to play with." Denise put her arms around J.R.'s neck. "Are you going to stand guard around this punch table, or are we going to party a little?"

"Yeah, let's party a little." J.R. winked at his friend, and went with Denise on the dance floor.

Sean kept his eyes on Denise and J.R. all night. He had been waiting for a chance to talk to Denise alone. Lisa had tried to get her to go to the restroom, but she wouldn't go. Now it seemed as if his luck may change. J.R. had put on his jacket, but it didn't seem as if Denise wanted to go. He should have known that. Denise would want to stay to the end, and so would Sean if it meant a chance to talk to her. Denise was holding on to J.R.'s arm.

"Aw, come on J.R., why would you want to leave now? It's not even late yet."

"Look Denise, if you want to stay, fine. Me, I've got a track meet tomorrow, and I intend to win." J.R. turned to his friend.

"Hey! Let me have two cups of punch. You know one for the road."

His friend poured one cup of punch and handed it to Denise. He picked up another cup that was already half full, and added some ice and a little more punch. He handed the second one to J.R., who took Denise around the shoulder and walked off to the side. Denise was pouting.

"I didn't say I wanted any punch."

"Oh just take a sip Denise, and stop being such a baby." Denise took a sip.

"Are you staying or what?"

"No, Denise. I think I'd better be going. But here, why don't you take this cup of punch over to Sean. He looks like he could use it, and I didn't drink out of it yet."

"Why would I do that?"

"Look, I'm leaving. You might as well have someone to dance with. Besides, we're on the same team. It'll kind of smooth the water between us. Plus, he's no threat to me. Here take it, yours has lipstick on it."

Denise looked at J.R. and then at Sean.

"O.K. I guess I might as well. I haven't really talked to Lisa all night."

"Good. See you tomorrow at the meet." He kissed her on her neck and forehead, and left.

Denise walked towards the table where Kevin and Lisa were sitting. Sean stood up to give her his seat. His palms were sweating.

"Hi. I brought you some punch."

"Thanks."

Sean took the cup from Denise. He was too excited to drink. Kevin and Lisa stopped talking.

"Denise, please take this man on the dance floor. He's been driving us crazy all night."

"He hasn't been doing too badly. I saw him dancing earlier."

Lisa held her head.

"Oh no, don't tell me you've been watching him, while he's been watching you!" They all laughed.

"Yeah Sean, put down that cup and go dance."

They both put their cups on the table and went to dance. Lisa and Kevin stayed and watched.

"Well, it's about time." Kevin remarked.

"You're not kidding. Let's have a toast. They reached for their cups, but they were both empty.

"Say, they won't be back for a while, we can drink theirs." Lisa reached for Denise's cup, and passed Sean's to Kevin. They toasted and drank a little. Kevin wrinkled up his nose, and pointed to the cup.

"This stuff tastes funny."

"Does it?" Lisa asked, as she reached for the cup. "Let me

taste it."

She took a sip. "Yeah it seems to have an aftertaste.

"Let's dance, Lisa. I think I've been sitting too long. I'm starting to feel restless.

"Yeah, I know what you mean. It seems awful warm all of a sudden."

Lisa and Kevin began to dance. By the second record Kevin felt himself getting lightheaded. Lisa looked a little flushed, and was holding her hair up off of her neck. As Kevin bent over to tell her that he needed to get some air, he blacked out and crashed to the floor. Lisa yelled for help and knelt down to loosen his collar. When she stood back up, she felt the room reeling, and then she passed out. The students behind her caught her just as she was going down. Everyone was trying to figure out what was going on. The security guard came over and cleared the area, and radioed for help. Sean was holding Kevin's head. He could hear Denise screaming in the background, but he couldn't get himself to leave his friend.

The ambulance arrived and took them to the hospital. As the ambulance pulled off, Sean saw Darryl pull up. He yelled to the guard that Kevin's brother was here, and the two of them ran to the car. The guard told Darryl what he knew, and that there was no answer at their house. Darryl told the guard the name of the restaurant where their parent's were, and said he would meet them at the hospital. He told Sean to get in the car.

"Come on Sean, pull yourself together. We may be in for a long night."

"But they were fine, Darryl one minute they were dancing, the next minute, they were on the floor. I don't understand. What's going on?"

"We won't know the answer to that until the doctors examine them. But, I've some more bad news for you."

"Oh no. I thought it was freaky the way you pulled up like that."

"Yeah. I was coming to get you."

"Why? Is it Jesse?" Sean could hardly talk.

"It's Jesse, but it's a whole lot more."

"Talk, Darryl."

"O.K. but you've got to try to calm down. I tried to reach Jesse all afternoon and there wasn't any answer. I decided to drive by the house. Jesse's car was there, and the front door was open." Darryl paused.

"Come on Darryl, what is it? What happened? Where's Jesse? Is he alright?" Sean had grabbed Darryl's arm.

"They beat him Sean. They beat him bad, and he had lost a lot of blood by the time I got there. His jaw, his nose, some ribs, his head, man I'm sorry. It looks like they shot him with his own gun. I think they left him for dead. He could barely talk, but he was afraid they would come after you next."

Sean broke down and cried. Lisa, Kevin and now Jesse, too. He felt like his whole world was coming down around him. Sean thought about what Coach had told him about coming up against these walls. Sometimes it seems like you just can't take anymore, but somehow, you endure. He looked at Darryl.

"What else did he say?"

"Not as much as he wanted to. He was in a lot of pain. But, he said we were the only other family you have to look after you." Darryl watched Sean's face. "He said nobody knows, but you're really my little brother. He said it's time you knew, and not to let anybody hurt you."

Sean stopped crying. He stared at Darryl with his mouth open.

"Was he delirious?"

"No Sean, I don't think so."

They were at the hospital emergency entrance.

"Oh Mama. I've got to call Mama, and let her know."

"She's probably already here, Sean. I called her before I came to get you."

When they got inside, Mrs. Wilkes was hugging Lisa's mother and J.R. was leaning against a wall, as white as a sheet. Lisa and Kevin were still being examined. Sean asked at the desk for his brother. They told him he was

unconscious and that his mother was with him now. Sean
went down the hall to the room the nurse had given him.
He took a deep breath and pushed open the door. Louise
and Mr. Wilkes were standing by Jesse's bed talking. He
was heavily bandaged and had tubes and monitors all
around.

He looked at the two adults. Louise came over and
hugged Sean.

"Are you alright?"

"I'm O.K Mama. How's Jesse?"

"We're not sure, honey. We just don't know yet."

Sean looked at Mr. Wilkes, and then at his mother.

"Mama, have you met Mr. Wilkes?"

Louise looked at Mr. Wilkes, he nodded, and turned back
to Sean.

"Yes Sean. We've met. We met a long time ago."

"Is it true Mama? Is what Jesse told Darryl true?"

"I don't know, Sean. What did Jesse tell Darryl?"

"He said my father isn't really dead. That...that Darryl is
my brother..."

"And that Mr. Wilkes is your father. Yes Sean, it's true. I
didn't realize that this was the Mr. Wilkes you have been
talking about. I know you have a lot of questions, for both of
us, but let's wait until we can sit down and really talk."

They agreed. At that moment one of Jesse's monitors went
dead. The doctors flew in the room, ordered everybody out,
and began working over Jesse. In the hallway, Mrs. Wilkes
announced that they had just brought Kevin and Lisa out,
and that they had found some kind of drug in their systems,
but that they would be alright.

"It seems someone put something in their punch and they
both had a reaction. We intend to get to the bottom of it
tomorrow. " Lisa's mother said.

J.R. looked terrified.

"Sean, Kevin is asking for you. He's right down the hall."
Darryl showed him the way. "How's it going in there?"

"Not too good. The doctors put us out."

"How is your mother holding up?"

"She's trying to be strong. I guess for me."

Darryl put a hand on Sean's shoulder. "You've been through a lot today Sean, but you're doing fine. Keep the faith. Jesse will pull through."

"Thanks, Darryl. Thanks for being there for Jesse." Sean went into Kevin's room.

Sean forced himself to smile. "Hey man, that was some dance step you did out there. What do you do? Make them up as you go?!" Both boys laughed.

"Aw, Sean, don't make me laugh. I feel like I've been tortured."

The boys talked for a while. Kevin made Sean promise to win the trophy for him since he wouldn't be able to race. Meanwhile Darryl approached his father and Louise.

"So I guess this is like a family reunion for you two." He looked at his father right in the eyes. "Are there any more long lost family members out there running around tracks? A sister perhaps, doing the 440?"

Mr. Wilkes looked back into Darryl's eyes. He could tell he was upset. Maybe more disappointed in him than anything else. "Whoa Darryl, don't be disrespectful. I just found out about this tonight myself."

Darryl turned to Louise. "You mean you've been raising Sean all by yourself, and telling him his father was dead because you wanted to?"

"Not because I wanted to Darryl. That's just the way it worked out. There is more to the situation than doing what I might have wanted to do."

"No, it seems to me that you both did what you wanted to do, and that's why Sean is here today. I don't get it Dad. Why don't men respect their women, and their wives?"

"You really don't know the whole story Darryl. Your mother and I were having serious problems back then, and we both did some things we regretted. I'm not making excuses, but don't be so judgmental without all the facts."

"Don't get me wrong Dad, I can handle it. It's not cool in my book, but I can deal with it. I just hope Mom can deal with it when she finds out. Hey, you talk about problems, man you ain't seen nothing yet!" Darryl turned and walked away. Louise looked at Mr. Wilkes.

"He has a point. Your wife is not going to be too pleased to hear about this."

"Yeah, I know. But I'll have to face that on my own. I just wish you had said something before now. You knew how to reach me."

"And you knew how to reach me. Let's not talk about it now. I need to get Sean home."

Mr. Wilkes went into Kevin's room and told Sean that his mother was waiting for him. The doctors had done what they could for Jesse, and all they could do now was wait. He told Sean to go on home with his mother and he would pick them up in the morning for the track meet.

The next morning when Sean got to the locker room, the place was buzzing. Everyone was asking about Kevin and Lisa. They were also trying to figure out what Coach and the principal were doing with J.R. in Coach's office. Finally, Coach explained what was going on. J.R and his friend had confessed to spiking Sean's drink, so that he would be disqualified for using drugs. They never thought Kevin and Lisa would drink it instead. This meant that J.R was now off the team, suspended and could face criminal charges. Coach was depending now on Sean to take up the slack. Sean was shocked. He dropped his bag and made a move towards J.R.

"No Sean, we're not having any of that nonsense in here. I know you're upset. You're not the only one upset. So, get control of yourself. We need you now more than ever."

J.R. slipped out of the room, and the others started to calm down.

Coach gave the team a pep talk. "We don't have much time to warm up guys. You know what I expect, so let's get out there and win the title." Everyone let out a whooping yell and headed for the track. Coach stopped Sean.

"Sean, I heard about your brother. I'm praying for him."
"Thanks Coach. He needs it."

The runners lined up at the starter's line of the state championship. Sean thought about all the walls he'd run hrough to get to this point. He had run from gangs and prostitutes, his brother, Denise, his mother and the city. He looked at the runners and missed Kevin. He even missed .R. How was his team going to win without two of its top runners? He thought about Kevin and Jesse and dedicated .he race to his brothers. Then, he thought of J.R. and how he would have loved to kick dust in the face of his archrival.

Sean looked around the stadium and saw his mother and Darryl. The gun was shot and the race began. Three miles and this wall would be history. It was a nice fall day, one lap around the track and into the park. Four hundred runners all wanted to win the race. The team prize going to the team that had the first five runners.

Coach had told the four other runners to stay close together and told Sean if he was in the top ten, they still may win, without J.R. and Kevin. Sean appeared to be floating, his mind seemed to be elsewhere while his body was running like a gazelle. The biggest race of the year and two of my brothers are in the hospital, my assistant coach became my father last night and I don't know where Denise is.

The runners re-entered the stadium. Sean and another runner were neck and neck for the lead after two and three quarter miles. Coach and Mr. Wilkes were hollering "You can do it." The crowd went wild as Sean lunged across the finish line first.

That afternoon Lisa and Kevin were released from the hospital. They were excited about Sean and the team's victory.

Jesse had pulled through, and would have to face criminal charges when he was released. But, he probably would not have to go to jail. Louise was going to move into Jesse's house to help out for a while. Sean felt pretty good.

"Things are working out huh, Mama?"

"Yes, things have a way of doing that."

"I even ended up with a father out of all this mess. The only problem is that, whenever things seem to be going well, something bad always seems to happen, and mess things up."

"Honey don't let that stop you from feeling good. You should know by now that everything happens for a reason. If it doesn't seem fair, that's O.K., it's still a part of life."

Denise walked into the hallway from the elevator. Louise noticed her first and nodded her head.

"Now, here comes another part of your life." Louise teased.

"Yes, but that's one of those good parts." Sean smiled at Denise.

"Hello, Mrs. Bradley.

"Hello, Denise."

"Hi, Sean. Congratulations on the race. Can I treat you to dinner to celebrate?

"Of course." He turned to his mother.

"Mom?"

"Bye. I'll meet you here later."

Sean and Denise walked to the elevators. Louise let out a deep sigh. Yes, things have a way of working out.

Denise and Sean went to a soul food restaurant. Denise apologized for her behavior with J.R.

"I guess I'm just so used to having my own way. When you acted like you weren't interested, it really hurt my feelings. I mean no one has ever rejected me like you did."

"Denise, I wasn't rejecting you. I just believe that relationships should be more than just sex. People have to spend time getting to know each other, and you never know who you may be talking to when you meet someone. You might become friends and then find out that you are related.

Believe me, your coming to the hospital today to be with me now, means more to me than any quick fling on the couch. Especially after you finding out the truth about where I was living and everything."

"Yeah, I think I know what you're saying Sean. I guess I've never met anyone who actually meant it like you do. Usually that's just a line some of the guys use, but I know you really mean it. And to be truthful, I'm glad you were strong enough to stand by your beliefs. Deep inside I guess I've been waiting to meet someone who really appreciates me for who I am, and not what I have or what I look like."

Sean grinned, "Really? Well stick with me baby." He leaned over and kissed her. "We've only just begun."

QUESTIONS FOR DISCUSSION

What is your opinion about Jesse's rationale to sell drugs?

What are the advantages and disadvantages of inner city and suburban schools?

How did you feel about Sean's mother letting him stay with Jesse and not telling him about his father?

What were the "walls" Sean had to face?

What "walls" are you up against?